JOURNAL TO INTIMACY
A GUIDED JOURNAL FOR SUSTAINING LOVE

ROSE OFFNER

This Book Belongs to

_____

&

_____

CELESTIALARTS
Berkeley, California

Love is patient
Love is kind
It does not envy
It does not boast
It is not proud
It is not rude
It is not self-seeking
It is not easily angered
It keeps no record of wrongs
Love does not delight in evil,
but rejoices in the truth,
it always protects,
always trusts,
always hopes,
always perseveres
Love never fails.

I Corinthians 13

Acknowledgments

To my mother, Casia Ruiz, whose love, support, and belief in my work lifts my spirits when I am weary, and who dries my tears when I am overwhelmed. Thanks for reminding me 'of course' I can do it! I love you, Mom. And to her dear friend Rich, for always listening when things are hard.

To Rick Bowman, my loving soul mate, whose love and persistence awakened my heart. I was searching for my 'type,' until the day he said to me, 'I may not be your type, but I am your balance.' Thank you for your support and making me feel safe.

A special thanks to all the couples who so generously shared their time, their challenges, and their inspirations of lasting love:

David and Audrey Levington, Mike and Janet Borges, Aaron and Elisia Parnell, Gina and Aaron Ruiz, Robert Ruiz and Shantel O'Neill, Karen and Fred Jonke.

Thanks to Marie and John Davies for permission to use their wedding photo, and to Amy and Steven Taddei for modeling.

Special thanks to Cathleen Carr, photographer and author of *Polaroid Transfers*, for the art lesson.

I am very grateful to the good people at the Cypress Inn at Half Moon Bay in Northern California for allowing us to photograph one of their rooms.

My dear friend Peter Scarsdale, thanks for taking the time to brainstorm with me. You are so smart, I love you.

Janna Bennett, kindred spirit, I adore you. You always make me laugh when I need it most.

My sister, Trish Smith, for your help when I really needed it. I love you.

To all my dearest friends and soul mates: Anne Taddei, Wendy McLaughlin, Lois Arrigotti, Debi Fernandez, Susan Sands, Margaret Phillips, Colleen Holden, Trudy Totty, Wendy & Tom Hubbard, Lori Cuevas. Without your belief in me, I could never have pulled it off.

Linda Mead, my agent extraordinaire, for your constant support and encouragement.

To my publishers, David Hinds and Phil Wood, thanks for giving me the opportunity to create this book.

Veronica Randall, editorial and art director, thanks for your valuable creative input, and thanks to Mary Ann Anderson, production manager, for your time and patience.

I am truly thankful to Robert Welsh of One Spirit Book Club. Your help has made a significant difference in my life and in the lives of many others.

Thank you, all of you, who call me, write to me, and buy and share my books with others. We are kindred spirits. Your calls and letters mean more than you know. Together, beginning with ourselves and our families, our love will make the world a better place.

And to Jo Ann Deck, my editor, for joining me in the education of the heart. As we pondered the questions in this book, our relationships became more tender, and we were filled with a new sense of appreciation for our partners.

Without the Holy Spirit, this book would not have been possible. It was a creation of love and divine inspiration, a gift from God. May we all love well and have the ability to weather our heart storms with grace and compassion.

Contents

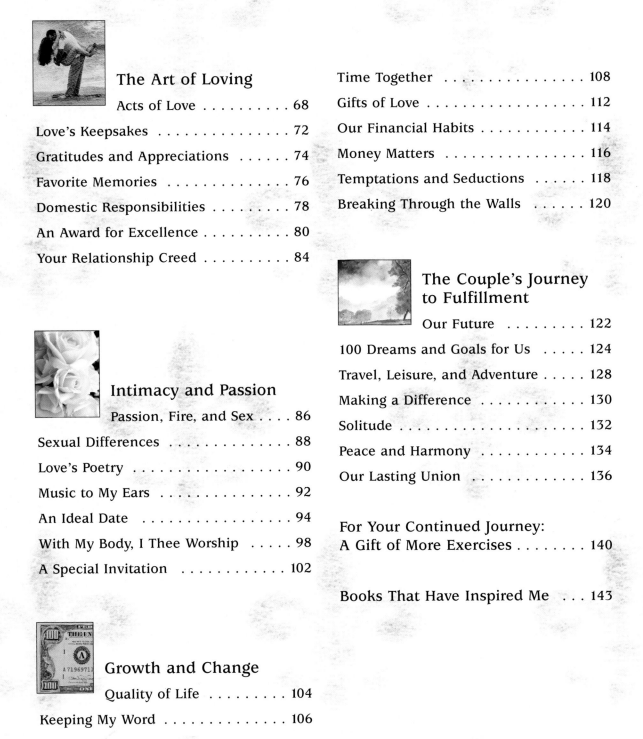

Once Upon a Time...Rose's Story

Once upon a time, there was a dark-haired girl with dark eyes, the eldest in a large family. She was raised by a loving mother and a mean stepfather. She was very angry at her stepfather for many years, for most of her adult life. One day she realized that not forgiving him had cost her a lot, because as long as she remained angry with him she was angry with all men. After many years of anguish she decided to forgive him and move on with her life. Part of her decision came from becoming a parent herself, and realizing that in parenting, mistakes are inevitable. She forgave him and confided her feelings to him. He cried and hugged her. At that moment, she could feel his love. Within days of their conversation, he fell ill and died. Her heart was at peace, having had the opportunity to make amends before it was too late.

Time passed and her anger dissipated. It never fully disappeared, just diminished until it was the size of a very small flame, just the perfect amount of anger, enough to protect her when she needed it. Though she hardly ever needed it anymore, it was somehow comforting to know it was still there.

She slowly became more of a woman, a woman who followed her dreams and faced her fears. She wrote books hoping she might help others to heal. And as she did, she too was healed.

One day she looked up and saw a big yellow harvest moon hanging low in the sky. It felt so close, like it was trying to come right into her home. She loved this big yellow moon. Somehow being alone with the moon reminded her about love, and she began to open her heart to the men she met. Suddenly there were many men in her life, and several pursued her to distant regions.

Though many men had loved her, she had never met the One, the one she could trust, the one who would be true to her, the one she felt safe with. A very tender man caught her attention. Though she was busy and difficult to catch, he tried gently and persistently to win her affection. He was a simple man, a common man, yet maybe not so common at all. In fact, his heart was made of pure gold, and she could see it glistening when she looked into his eyes. Animals loved him and nature was his second home. Through all his acts of kindness, she began to see the wonders of his loving heart.

Many of her dreams had been fulfilled and she had even realized her dream of having her writings published, but she was still not living the life she had imagined. She felt it was very near, almost within her grasp. And so she continued to work as hard as she could, and on those nights when she waitressed, he brought her dinner. It seemed she was always so busy going from one job to the next job, she rarely had time to stop. He began to cook for her so that she could write. He said 'Your writing is so important. You've helped so many people. Now let me help you.'

Though he was a good and kind man, still she felt herself resisting love's call. One day, as she sat reflect-ing on this, she found a tiny scrap of paper on which she had written the qualities she wanted in her soul mate. It said that he would be her best friend, her lover, a family man, and would have an outgoing nature, masculine energy, responsibility, and maturity. He would have a strong spiritual foundation or a good heart. They would have sexual chemistry. He would be successful in his own right, an adventurer, a thinker. She began to wonder if her current lover could be 'the one,' but he didn't seem to match all the pictures she had carried in her mind and heart.

Could they live happily ever after? She was tired of tripping over brambles and finding locked doors. She needed a map to the heart, a guide to help her through the maze. At the time, she was writing a couple's journal, and when it was finished, she would share it with him. Together they would ask and answer questions, find the treasures buried within each other, and explore the many regions of the heart.

Introduction: The Heart of the Matter

Journal to Intimacy is a couple's journal, a unique creation for nurturing love. You and your partner are invited to share your written words, strengthen your relationship, and keep a chronicle of your life together.

This book acts as a map with guided exercises that lead you through seven essential aspects of love. Asking questions of ourselves and each other stirs our souls and expands our hearts. We grow closer to those we love by sharing our true selves and expressing our vulnerability. Intimate sharing evokes tears and laughter and creates closeness and a deeper friendship.

I created this journal not because I am an expert but because I am a woman who desires love. I wanted a tool to help myself and others to sustain love and to guide us to a safe place where we could express our feelings to our partners.

During months of research, men shared with me their fears of intimacy. They said they were afraid of getting hurt, because their previous relationships had ended poorly. They said they needed help, but were afraid to trust. They wanted to learn better ways to express love, and they didn't know how. Some men said that they were afraid to love deeply because they feared that their vulnerability would cause them to lose power over women.

Many women told me that although their partners said that they loved them, their relationships lacked intimacy. They wanted a deeper emotional connection but they did not know how to create that closeness.

Our quest for happiness often depends on finding and sustaining love. True love implies commitment. Before you begin this journal, it is important to ask yourself the following questions. First of all, do you and your partner call yourselves a couple? If not, is it appropriate to be doing this work? You might also ask yourself how do you define husband, wife, relationship, marriage, or commitment. I have heard couples refer to each other as 'my husband' or 'my wife' long before they were married, because they had agreed in their hearts and a union had been made. I also heard a writer say of her first marriage, that 'he' was not her husband. Sometimes couples are married forever and have not yet become 'husband' and 'wife.' We must all explore these words with each other and in our own hearts.

Each relationship teaches us and deepens our perception of love. In our hearts, we carry a piece of each person we have loved. Love has many degrees. As you explore your feelings, you may discover that you and your partner are at different levels. Since love cannot be forced, this is the time to practice a prayer of acceptance. Recognize the valuable gifts you have learned from each other and remember that there is a middle ground, a place where you can meet and ask for a resolution that would be for the highest good of all concerned. Trust that life works, and that a greater plan exists for all of us.

JOURNAL TO INTIMACY uses romantic images, color, art, and metaphor to nourish the soul. All who worked on this book blessed it, and we pass those blessings on to you. Although you could open to any page and begin at random, self-inquiry is a powerful place to start. Often the issues we blame on others are the ones we have with ourselves.

SELF-INQUIRY is the practice of honest examination. We ask ourselves the questions we have about life and find our own answers. Until we have experienced self-love and made peace with ourselves, it is difficult to have healthy, loving relationships. Self-inquiry is soul work, and leads us on the path of authenticity. We write about our journey to love, our values, our challenges, and what we've learned. We face our fears and come up with acts of courage. Self-exploration gives us the opportunity to find and be ourselves.

FROM ANGER AND HURT TO FORGIVENESS is the essential process in which relationships are tested, where we learn, grow, and love. Being a couple is hard work. Conflicts will happen. Anger and frustration often have a long history that can follow us until we face our deepest hurts. It is in our intimate relationships where we learn to forgive and be forgiven. Forgiveness is the act of letting go of our grievances. At times some issues seem unforgivable; we must learn to practice forgiveness on a daily basis. True forgiveness means that all our anger has been released and we do not need to mention it again. Facing pain and anger with courage helps us to weather the storms of the heart.

COMMUNICATION is the key to developing intimacy in our relationships. Couples don't, won't, and can't always agree. Disagreements happen, problems will arise. Emotional growth occurs when we begin to practice letting go of having to be right. Talking, listening, hearing, acknowledging, and validating each other's feelings creates intimate sharing. We feel loved when we know that our feelings are heard, remembered, and honored.

Often all we really want is not advice or answers, but simply to be heard. Being emotionally present is the practice of listening without interrupting or disengaging. Mutual respect develops as we let go of criticism, blame, and the need to make each other wrong. We express our frustrations, forgive each other's shortcomings, and encourage self-improvement.

Silence is also a form of communication. For many couples, what is unspoken is as important as what is spoken. Paying attention to our partner's subtle nuances, verbal and nonverbal, shows that we respect their feelings. Words that go unexpressed get stuck in our bodies and over time, dis-ease is created, leaving the soul restless. When we know that there is nothing left unsaid, we can experience peace in our lives.

THE ART OF LOVING allows us to let down our walls, those hard and distant places inside us begin to disappear and we can create a passionate union. Love grows and the heart expands through thoughtful actions and behaviors, gratitude and appreciation. Loving partners deserve awards and praise. Continual acts of love, large and small, create intimacy. Intimacy deepens as we define and renew our vows. We are transformed from being seekers and finders of love, to becoming the source of love.

Love is a verb. Our daily practice builds intimacy. The son of a minister once said that a thousand acts of love are not enough. Developing intimacy takes ten thousand acts of love.

INTIMACY AND SEX are not the same, although through sex you can experience intimacy and bliss. While passion is the fire that ignites our connection to our partner, intimacy grows through deep and honored sharing. When a couple experiences intimacy and passion, their eyes speak a silent language of love. Passion grows and deepens when we are active and happy. We can create fire through loving gestures that show our partner the depth of our care.

GROWTH AND CHANGE can be inspired by true love, making us into better people. In our relationships our strengths and weaknesses come to light. Change often happens when something in our relationship is no longer working. Many men and women who have been married more than once experience growth and change after a relationship ends. They are then inspired to work on improving themselves. Challenges call us to self-improvement. Yet we need not jeopardize our relationship by waiting to change.

Committed couples grow together. They desire to make their partners happy. They know that if their partner is happy, they will be happier, too.

Successful couples who have long histories together have grown and developed a willingness to make changes to improve themselves, their relationships, and the quality of their lives. The pursuit of their shared interests as well as maintaining their individual interests keeps them passionate about life. Growing and developing enhances our ability to sustain love and intimacy. As we ask for change, we must also be willing to change ourselves. Keeping a shared journal gives you a tool for practicing exercises that allow you to let go of your resistance to change.

THE COUPLE'S JOURNEY TO FULFILLMENT is the expression of a love that has deepened and matured. The heart has grown in its capacity to love and serve others. The practice of loving kindness has become our chosen expression. We have relinquished our fears of intimacy and embraced emotional communion. We continue to release any thoughts of the need to dominate or control our partner. We have given each other the freedom to be ourselves. We experience fulfillment as we create our dreams and make a difference in the lives around us. The practice of extending compassion leads us to inner peace.

Instructions for Heart and Soul

The guided exercises in *Journal to Intimacy* act as a foundation for building a spiritual union. Before you start any exercise, begin with a silent prayer. Call upon God, spirit, your guardian angel; invoke the divine.

Journal keeping can be both transformative and scary. Vulnerability can bring forth tears. If you cry, don't be afraid. It is our resistance to our emotions that keeps us stuck. Stay with your feelings. Dry your eyes and keep your hand moving. Begin to recall the truth. Facing the truth shines light on the dark places in our hearts, diminishing their power. Acknowledging and writing the truth is an exercise in liberation and leads us to acceptance and understanding. Expressing yourself allows the process of compassionate healing to begin.

How to Begin

You may be excited to begin this journal only to find your partner unwilling or resistant. Do not lose faith—begin by yourself. Shared written communication often opens the door for verbal communication. You might find yourself lying in bed sharing what you've written with your partner. This kind of intimate sharing will enhance your relationship and that is the intention of this journal. Your intentionality holds power. Love will find its own way.

If your partner does not like to write, ask the question and record their answer. This way you will remember what your partner has said and you can reread their words. The key is to develop intimate sharing, written or spoken, and to let love grow. All relationships are unique. Each couple must face their own challenges and issues. If you cannot relate to a certain exercise, please refer to the back of this book to the section called 'More Exercises,' where you can select a more appropriate question.

I interviewed many couples while researching this book, and asked those who had been married for a long time how and why they had succeeded. Some shared with me that at one time they had thought of separating but had gone for couple's counseling instead. They learned valuable communication skills that helped them stay together and enhanced their relationship. Love is a decision. If you think that you and your partner might need counseling, I would strongly encourage you to seek it out. Many of the healthiest people I know have gone for counseling when they needed it.

Many counselors encourage journal-keeping. I also recommend that you keep your own private journal to maintain your individuality, as some parts of our lives are private and should not be shared.

Journal to Intimacy will inspire curiosity, so find both a safe and convenient place to keep it. Write directly over the art. If you make a mistake, keep writing. Some of our greatest life lessons have come from what seemed like mistakes. Mistakes are inevitable. You may find yourself reluctant to write in this journal because of the art, but your written word on top of the art enhances the images and makes the pages look even more beautiful. You deserve to write in something beautiful. It will remind you of your own worth.

In keeping a shared journal, remember to leave half the writing space for your partner. Before each exercise, preview the number of pages and write only on your half. If an exercise has four pages, two are for you and two are for your partner. If you need more space, continue on with another sheet of paper and create a pocket at the back of the book to save those pages.

If you tend to ramble when you write, simply ask yourself, 'What am I trying to say?' and then say it. Brevity brings us to the heart of the matter.

Decorating Your Journal

You are invited to express yourself playfully. You can embellish your journal with gold stars, glitter glue, colored pens, collage, stickers, and Crayola Changeables™. Glue in pockets and envelopes of your own creation to save cherished cards and keepsakes. You can design a love letter pocket, an anger pocket, a place for unsent letters. In my journal, I've even created a pocket for saving favorite fortunes from fortune cookies that speak to my heart.

FOR YOUR CONTINUED JOURNEY: A GIFT OF MORE EXERCISES appears at the back of the book to encourage you to create your own couple's journal. You can begin with your own blank book, draw your own artwork, and write your own questions. My hope for you is that you will have a sacred place to express your love, fears, challenges, and desires.

May your relationship grow deep and rich in lasting love.

Rose Offner

True Love

Tell the story of how you met your partner. Begin with 'once upon a time,' or 'long, long ago.' Write about why you were attracted to each other. Express how you have fulfilled each other's longing, needs, and desires. Describe the obstacles you overcame. Create a happy ending for your future together.

Once upon a time ... to be continued

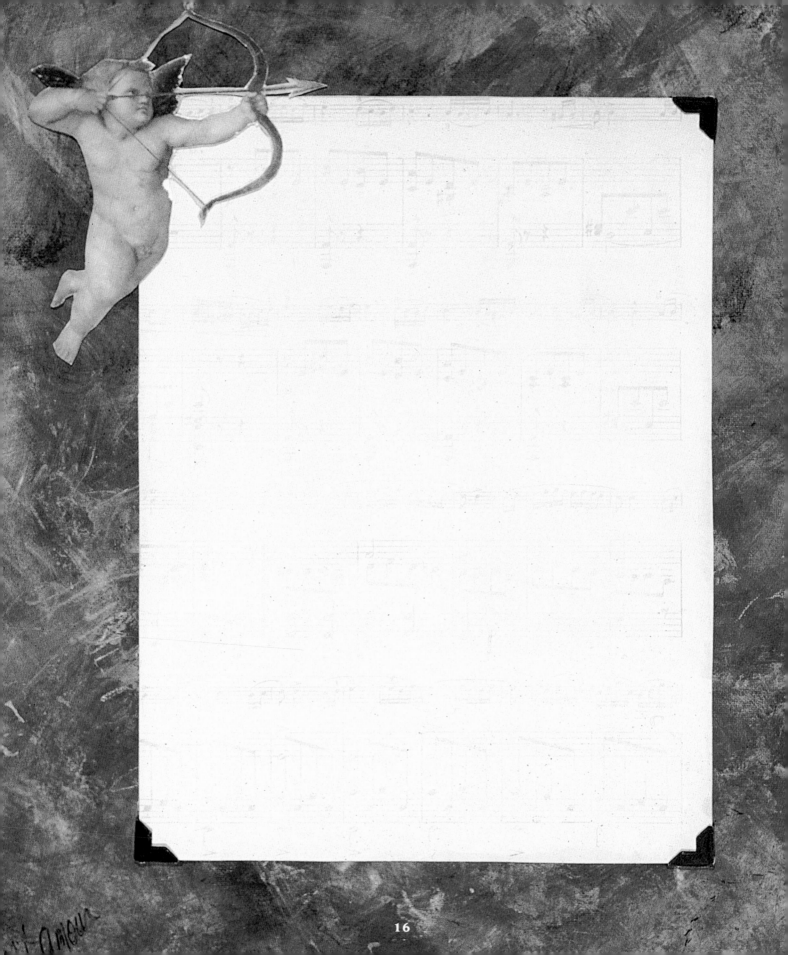

MONEY

FAMILY

INTEGRITY

GENEROSITY

EDUCATION

SELF-DISCIPLINE

MUTUAL RESPECT

Values

Values are the principles that we hold most important in life. They help us to clarify our purpose and establish direction. When we honor our values, we are much happier with ourselves. List your top ten values. Compare your list with your partner. Often when couples experience difficulties, it's not because they don't love each other or share interests together, but because their values are different. For example, some people say that they value family but don't spend time nurturing their family relationships, and thus conflict arises. Express how both your shared and different values affect the nature of your relationship.

SPIRITUALITY   FRIENDSHIP   RESPONSIBILITY

HEALTH   LEADERSHIP   PERSONAL GROWTH

FREEDOM

INDIVIDUALITY

COMPASSION

PEACE

EQUALITY

CREATIVITY

NATURE

ADVENTURE

TAKING RISKS   HARD WORK   HUMOR   TRUTH

What I've Learned About Relationships

We learn by example. Describe what you've learned about relationships from your parents or caregivers. What loving acts do you remember? What negative situations still trouble you?

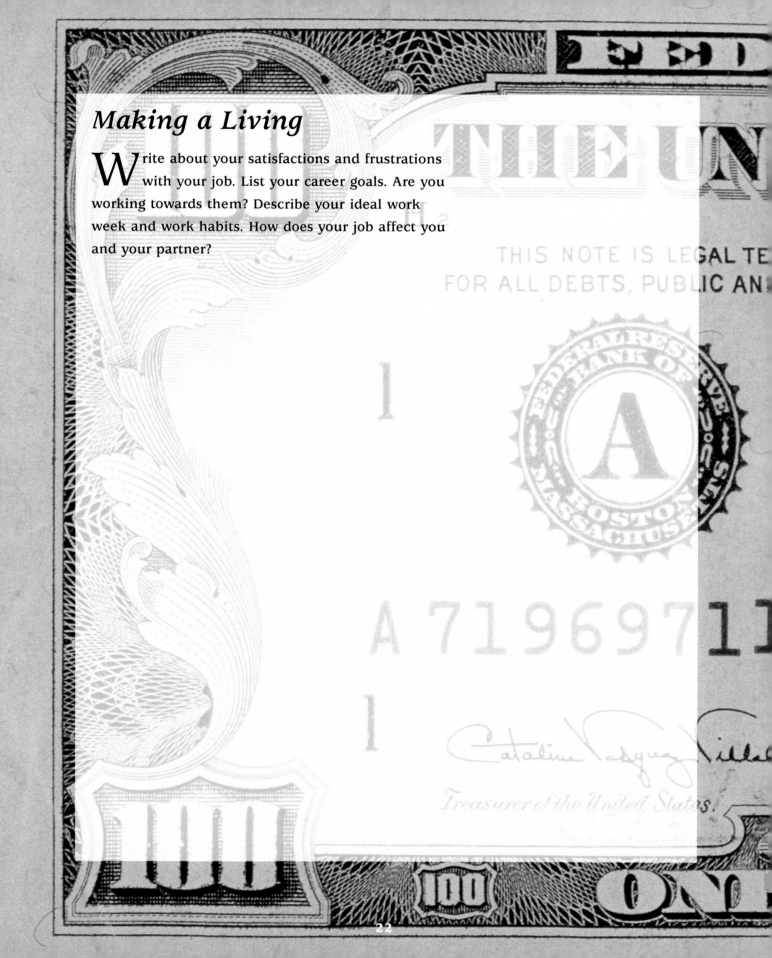

Making a Living

Write about your satisfactions and frustrations with your job. List your career goals. Are you working towards them? Describe your ideal work week and work habits. How does your job affect you and your partner?

Our Fears

Our fears—known and unknown, real and imagined—inhibit intimacy. Naming our fears often diminishes their power over us. Create a list of your fears and share them. Explore how they prevent closeness.

Acts of Courage

Acts of courage strengthen your will and assist you in developing a brave heart. Taking action moves you through your fears and helps you gain personal power. List the actions you would be willing to take to break through your fears.

Family Challenges:
Yours, Mine, Ours

Within each challenge is an opportunity for growth. Write about your current family struggles: parents, in-laws, children, other relatives, and how they are affecting your life and relationship.

Distance and Closeness

Whenever you withdraw in a relationship, you grow apart. What causes you to withdraw? Explain the issues that create emotional distance. Tell your partner what you need in order to reconnect.

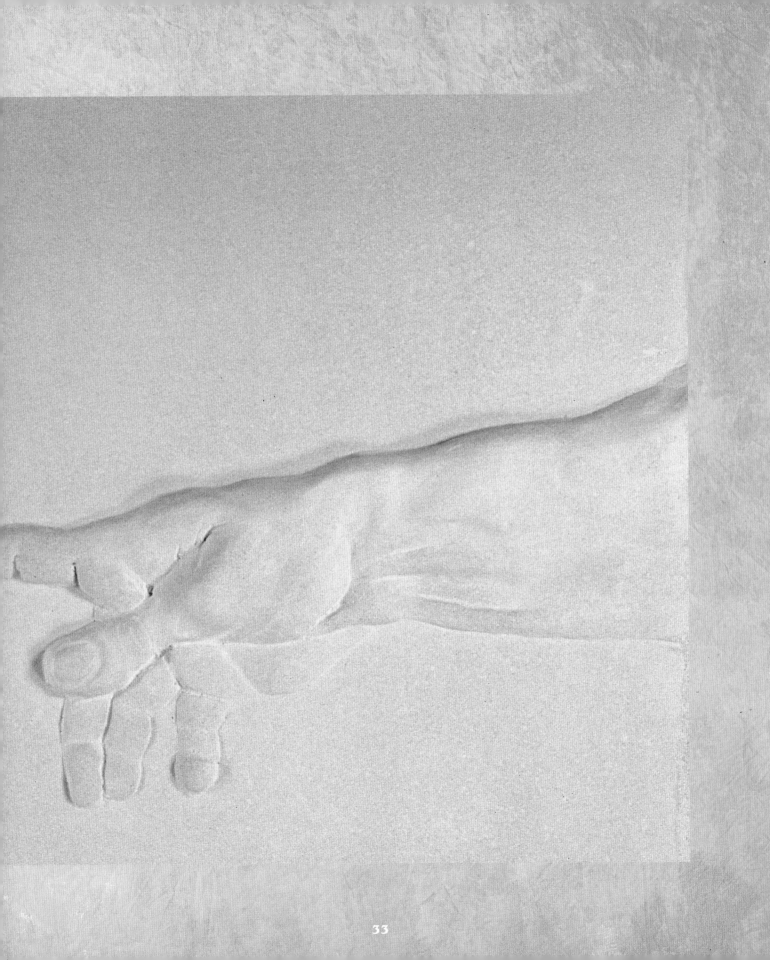

Hurtful Behaviors

What actions or behaviors are frustrating your partner? Pay attention to your partner's complaints and requests. How could you be more respectful of each other's feelings? List behaviors that you need to change. Create new ways to give and take.

Criticism: A Deadly Relationship Sin

One of the easiest ways to destroy love is through criticism. Observe your behavior. Identify the subtle ways you criticize, judge, or belittle your partner. Practice making amends for your disrespectful actions. What can you do to treat your partner with more respect?

I'm So Sorry

Sometimes we hurt the people we love, consciously or unconsciously. Make amends to your partner by acknowledging your mistakes or wrongdoings. Explain what happened and ask for forgiveness. If action or compensation is necessary, develop a plan.

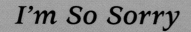

Green-Eyed Monster

Write about the things that make you uncomfortable or jealous. How can your partner help you overcome your feelings? Ask yourself if inappropriate behavior is affecting you and your relationship. Describe what makes you feel sensitive, such as extreme flirting.

Anger Process

This exercise can help you understand the origin and history of your anger. Often anger and resentments have their own stories.

• Think of a person you are angry with or who has hurt you, or of a difficult situation that you would like to have healed.

• Recall the situation or person clearly. Identify what the other person said or did and list the feelings this memory evokes. Were you hurt, scared, or frustrated?

• What did you do in that situation to stop taking care of yourself?

• What did you need to do in order to take care of yourself?

• Go back to your earliest recollection of when it first happened, or when you had the first feelings. Go back as far as you can, recalling if you had any childhood memories of these or similar feelings. Imagine yourself doing whatever you needed to do in order to take care of yourself. Anytime you feel anger, remember to ask yourself 'How am I not taking care of myself right now?' and do whatever you need to do to take care of yourself.

Extending Forgiveness

In a healthy relationship, forgiveness is a daily practice. Forgiveness is the act of letting go of our anger and grudges. When we remember that our partner loves us and would not intentionally hurt us, we can accept their apology with grace. Express your willingness to forgive your partner.

Sharing

Tell your partner what you are feeling. Your partner will never know unless you tell them. Begin with using the word 'I' instead of 'you.' You can say, 'I am angry,' or 'I am feeling resentment.' Whenever we use the word 'you,' such as 'You make me angry,' your partner feels attacked. Express the truth. Practice sharing your feelings by using 'I' statements.

I _____ when _____

because _____ .

Good Fortune

Our belief in ourselves and each other can move us to accomplish our dreams. Glue an envelope on this page and save your good fortunes from fortune cookies. Or write your own fortunes as affirmations or prayers for yourself and your relationship and glue them here.

Time and Place

S ome couples have chosen not to discuss sensitive
issues in the bedroom or during meals. Finding
the right time and place is vital for intimate sharing.
List the best time and place for you and your partner.
What else makes talking easier?

Communication Styles

I dentify the strengths and weaknesses in how you talk with each other. Do you communicate clearly and with respect, listening to your partner? Or do you interrupt, withdraw, argue, become defensive, or sarcastic? What prompts you to become dominant, controlling, passive, or aggressive? List how you can improve the ways you share your feelings and hear your partner.

Making Requests

Couples who love strive to please each other. Ask your partner for something you need, desire, or want to see changed. List your requests here. Your partner can now respond. When your partner has honored your requests, acknowledge and thank them. If you cannot honor each other's requests, practice acceptance and realize that some issues will resolve themselves with time.

Begin with 'I have a request...' or 'What I would like from you is...'

_____

_____

_____

The Response

_____

_____

_____

No More Words

An important aspect of communication is knowing when not to talk. It is hard to listen when we are tired, stressed, hungry, or watching television. Often what we really want is peace and quiet. List the times during the day when your partner runs out of words and can no longer hear you. Honor your partner's need for relaxation before making requests and asking a lot of questions. Write about how you can create the time to be fully present and give your full attention.

Questions from the Heart

Create an ongoing list of questions for your partner regarding love and intimacy. For example, what is a relationship? How do you define love and devotion? What are the qualities of a perfect partner? Give each other time to ponder the questions.

Acts of Love

Love is a verb. Once you know what makes your partner feel loved, you can initiate thoughtful actions
and loving behaviors. Create a list of what makes you feel
loved, special, cared about, and nurtured. Share your list
with your partner.

Love's Keepsakes

Create and design a love pocket to share and save the keepsakes of your relationship. Special cards, letters, concert or play tickets can go here.

Gratitudes and Appreciations

A simple thank-you goes a long way. Praise and appreciation creates a momentum of continued loving and helpful actions. Keep a list of your appreciation for your partner. Remember also to thank them verbally.

Favorite Memories

What are some of your favorite shared memories? Keep an ongoing list of cherished moments that you and your partner have experienced together.

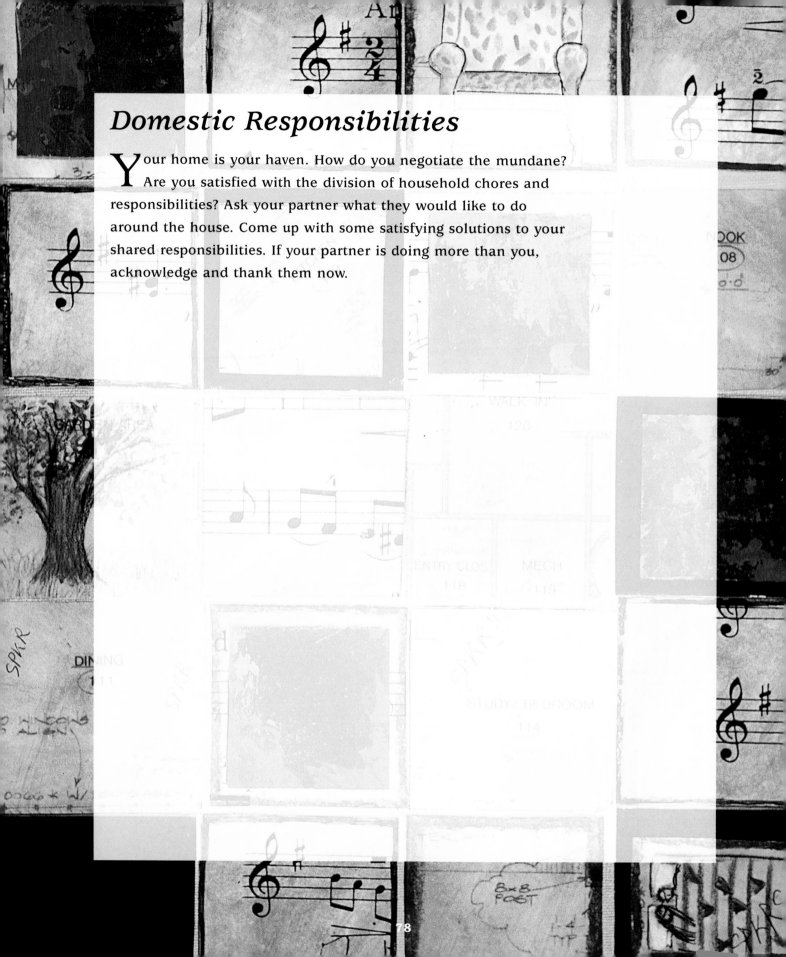

Domestic Responsibilities

Your home is your haven. How do you negotiate the mundane? Are you satisfied with the division of household chores and responsibilities? Ask your partner what they would like to do around the house. Come up with some satisfying solutions to your shared responsibilities. If your partner is doing more than you, acknowledge and thank them now.

An Award for Excellence

Give your partner an award for an outstanding accomplishment, an area of growth and improvement, or a job well done.

Certificate of Excellence

Awarded to _____

On This Day _____

For _____

Signed _____

I am proud of you!

Certificate of Excellence

Awarded to _____

On This Day _____

For _____

Signed _____

I am proud of you!

Certificate of Excellence

Awarded to _____

On This Day _____

For _____

Signed _____

I am proud of you!

Certificate of Excellence

Awarded to _____

On This Day _____

For _____

Signed _____

I am proud of you!

Your Relationship Creed

A creed expresses a deeply held belief. To help create a lasting union, write a sacred creed for your relationship, expressing your intentions and commitments to love, honor, and cherish your partner.

Passion, Fire, and Sex

Write about all the little things that excite you and lead to making love or feeling close, for example: holding hands, a subtle touch, a special look, laughter, playful banter. List and describe the romantic, intimate, and sexual things that you enjoy or wish would happen more often.

Sexual Differences

Write about your sexual differences. Describe those actions that affect your sexual mood and appetite. How do you, as a couple, work through this situation? Does your partner enjoy a form of sexual stimulation that you do not like? How can you, as a couple, satisfy each other's needs and desires? List creative solutions.

Love's Poetry

Express your love by writing your partner a poem,
love letter, or a special card of your own design.
Create your own envelope for these treasures and
paste it here.

Music to My Ears

Express terms of endearment and compliments that you enjoy hearing most from your partner, and those words of love that you would like to hear more often.

An Ideal Date

I magine and describe your most ideal date.
Create an ongoing list of romantic dates
or fun activities to share over time.

With My Body, I Thee Worship

A long time ago, English wedding vows included the words 'With my body, I thee worship.' Write about the sacred and holy nature of physical love. Describe the ways you can use your body to worship your partner and ignite passion. Create an atmosphere to encourage connection between body and soul, with candles, massage, music. Name other ways you can arouse the sensual nature of love.

A Special Invitation

Extended an invitation to your partner for a special date. Surround them with love and appreciation.

You're invited to:

_____

Place:

_____

Time:

_____

Date:

_____

P.S. Please bring:

Quality of Life

List your self-defeating habits, patterns, and behaviors. Describe how they affect your life and health. Name the positive actions and attitudes you can embrace. Express what you need to do for yourself and how you can help your partner.

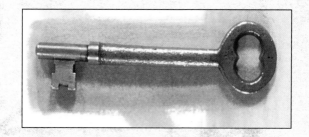

Keeping My Word

CONTRACT

I, _____, am committed to keeping my word with you.

I know that words hold power. I agree to: _____

_____.

I will keep my promise to you. As I keep this agreement, I know that I am

building a foundation of trust and integrity with you and with myself.

Signature:

Date:

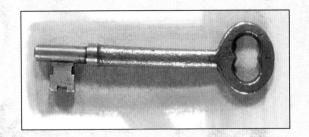

Keeping My Word

CONTRACT

I, _____, am committed to keeping my word with you.

I know that words hold power. I agree to: _____

_____.

I will keep my promise to you. As I keep this agreement, I know that I am

building a foundation of trust and integrity with you and with myself.

Signature:

Date:

Time Together

Spending time together builds intimacy. Respecting time spent alone or with friends is also a loving act. Decide how much time you can spend with each other without neglecting personal interests, friends, or family. Coordinate your calendars and plan your time together. List activities and social engagements to share over the next six months.

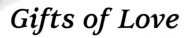

Gifts of Love

Gifts are an expression of love. Listen to what your partner asks for, desires, and needs. Notice what they don't have. Surprise them with a favorite meal, flowers, a massage, small necessary items. Begin a list of gifts for your partner. Remember the ultimate gift — time spent together. That is often the best gift of all.

Our Financial Habits

How do you and your partner handle financial responsibilities? How do you differ in your financial habits? How are you the same? Identify your difficulties with saving, spending, charging, and planning for the future. List the ways you and your partner can strengthen your security.

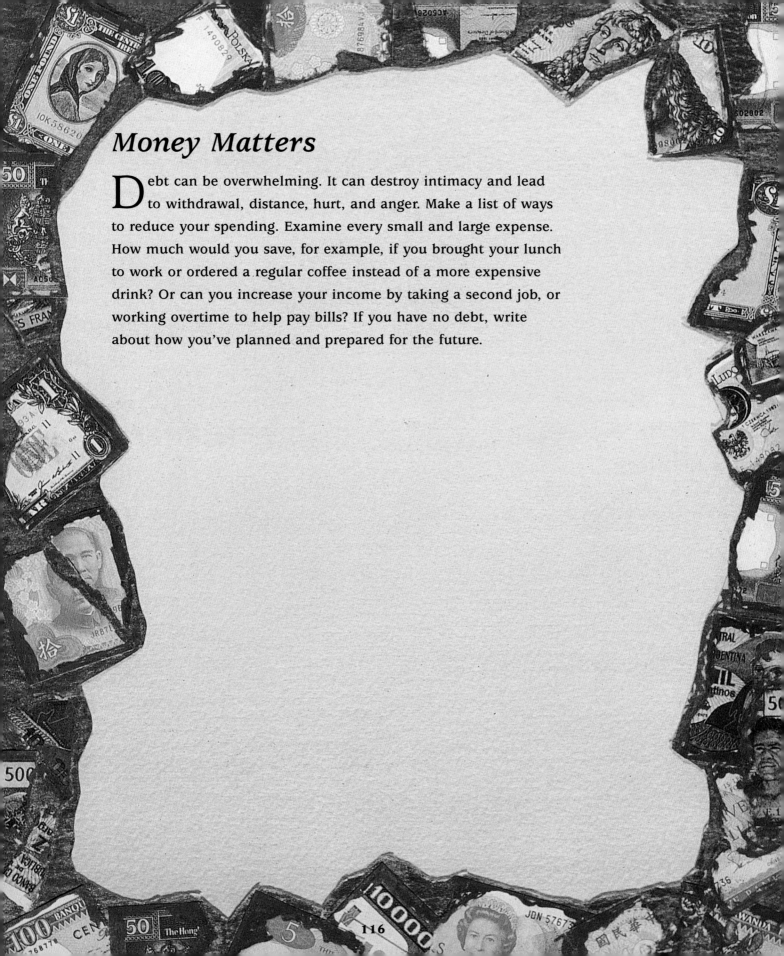

Money Matters

Debt can be overwhelming. It can destroy intimacy and lead to withdrawal, distance, hurt, and anger. Make a list of ways to reduce your spending. Examine every small and large expense. How much would you save, for example, if you brought your lunch to work or ordered a regular coffee instead of a more expensive drink? Or can you increase your income by taking a second job, or working overtime to help pay bills? If you have no debt, write about how you've planned and prepared for the future.

Temptations and Seductions

Although we love our partners, we will sometimes feel attracted to someone else. Such illusions can create confusion. When this happens, remember to give yourself time out and ask yourself, "What are the consequences?" Describe what you would do if you or your partner faced temptation, and how you would overcome it together.

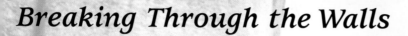

Breaking Through the Walls

To be defensive is the act of guarding oneself against aggression or attack. Being defensive in a relationship stifles growth, inhibits intimacy, and builds walls. List the issues, weaknesses, or personal flaws that cause you to guard yourself. Tell your partner your true feelings. Express your resentments with 'I' statements (I am angry, I feel scared) and let them know what you need.

Our Future

Visualization is a powerful way to create our desired life. Describe your ideal vision for your future together. In five, ten, and twenty years, where will you be living, working, and spending time?

100 Dreams and Goals for Us

List 100 dreams and desires, fifty for you and fifty for your partner. Write about your heart's yearnings; be specific about family and home, work and career, personal and spiritual goals, your dreams for your loved ones, and even your hopes for the world. To achieve what you desire in life, you must first know what you want. As your dreams are realized, remember to check them off. It is empowering to know that you can achieve your goals.

1. _____ ☐
2. _____ ☐
3. _____ ☐
4. _____ ☐
5. _____ ☐
6. _____ ☐
7. _____ ☐
8. _____ ☐
9. _____ ☐
10. _____ ☐
11. _____ ☐
12. _____ ☐
13. _____ ☐
14. _____ ☐
15. _____ ☐
16. _____ ☐
17. _____ ☐
18. _____ ☐
19. _____ ☐

20. _____ ☐
21. _____ ☐
22. _____ ☐
23. _____ ☐
24. _____ ☐
25. _____ ☐
26. _____ ☐
27. _____ ☐
28. _____ ☐
29. _____ ☐
30. _____ ☐
31. _____ ☐
32. _____ ☐
33. _____ ☐
34. _____ ☐
35. _____ ☐
36. _____ ☐
37. _____ ☐
38. _____ ☐
39. _____ ☐
40. _____ ☐
41. _____ ☐
42. _____ ☐
43. _____ ☐
44. _____ ☐
45. _____ ☐
46. _____ ☐

47. _____ ☐

48. _____ ☐

49. _____ ☐

50. _____ ☐

51. _____ ☐

52. _____ ☐

53. _____ ☐

54. _____ ☐

55. _____ ☐

56. _____ ☐

57. _____ ☐

58. _____ ☐

59. _____ ☐

60. _____ ☐

61. _____ ☐

62. _____ ☐

63. _____ ☐

64. _____ ☐

65. _____ ☐

66. _____ ☐

67. _____ ☐

68. _____ ☐

69. _____ ☐

70. _____ ☐

71. _____ ☐

72. _____ ☐

73. _____ ☐

74. _____ ☐
75. _____ ☐
76. _____ ☐
77. _____ ☐
78. _____ ☐
79. _____ ☐
80. _____ ☐
81. _____ ☐
82. _____ ☐
83. _____ ☐
84. _____ ☐
85. _____ ☐
86. _____ ☐
87. _____ ☐
88. _____ ☐
89. _____ ☐
90. _____ ☐
91. _____ ☐
92. _____ ☐
93. _____ ☐
94. _____ ☐
95. _____ ☐
96. _____ ☐
97. _____ ☐
98. _____ ☐
99. _____ ☐
100. _____ ☐

Travel, Leisure, and Adventure

How do you decide on your vacations and where to spend them? Plan some future trips and make a list of short- and long-term adventures you would like to experience, either alone or together.

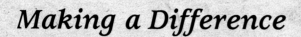

Making a Difference

In serving others we have the opportunity to give back the love that has been given to us. Love awakens us and motivates us to share ourselves with the world. What charities or causes inspire you to contribute?

Solitude

Everyone needs time alone, to relax and preserve our individuality. List the ways that you like to be alone. Describe what rejuvenates your soul. How can you accommodate your own and your partner's need to be alone?

Peace and Harmony

In times of disagreements and chaos, we often seek peace through beauty and nature. Peace includes freedom, security, and order. Write your own definition of peace. What areas of your life are out of control and are calling for your attention? How can you create more peace and harmony?

ROSE OFFNER

Our Lasting Union

How has your love grown richer over time? Mature love is less prone to anger and needing to be right. The desire to dominate and demand our own way has faded. Our acts of kindness to each other have become second nature. The union of our hearts has created a magnificent WE. Write an acknowledgment to your partner for the positive difference that they make in your life.

For Your Continued Journey:

A Gift of More Exercises

Every day we have a choice to journey to intimacy. Every day we continue to change and grow. Here are more exercises to help you to enhance and sustain your relationship.

Attraction

The strengths and abilities that attracted me to you and helped me feel complete are:

The strengths and abilities I am lacking and would like to acquire are:

Great Expectations

Define your expectations for romance, intimacy, and sex. How do these differ from your partner's? How does this affect your relationship?

Soul Mates

When you meet your soul mate or life partner, the real work begins. Create your own definition of a healthy couple.

Role Playing

Identify and describe the different roles you play in your life. Are you a critic, a judge, a controller, a child, or a perfectionist? What different roles do you play with your partner?

Temperament

Couples must learn to adjust to each other's moods. The ancient Greeks divided temperament into four basic types: sanguine (sunny/happy), melancholy (sensitive/sad), phlegmatic (slow/lazy), and choleric (aggressive/quick to anger). Which one of these describes you best? Are you a combination? Each disposition has positive and negative traits. Describe how you can seek balance within yourself and how you can support your partner in achieving balance.

Unfinished Business

Write about any unfinished business from your past that still affects your life, relationship, dreams, and peace of mind.

Inner Conflict

Inner conflicts can lead to outer conflicts. Which conflicts in your relationship are really about another issue?

Needs

Think about the times you feel hurt, distant, or unhappy. Often, we are frustrated when our needs and desires are not being met. Name your unfulfilled needs.

Feeling Safe

Tell your partner what you need to feel safe in your relationship. Describe what is necessary for you to feel safe, protected, secure, and stable.

Unresolvable Issues

Name the unresolvable issues in your relationship. Express how you can come to terms with these problems and how you can accept your partner.

Laughter and Love

Laughter is good for the soul. If you are not laughing enough, how can you bring more fun and lightness into your life together?

The Extra Steps

When we love, we go the extra mile. How does your partner go the extra mile for you? How do you go the extra mile for your partner?

Giving More

Make a list of the ways to give more of yourself to your partner.

I Promise

Make an ongoing list of promises to your partner and keep them.

Nature's Cycle

Relationships are cyclical in nature. Sometimes you feel close or distant, hot or cool. Describe the current cycle between you and your partner.

The Hard Times

Describe how your partner has stayed with you through the rough times. Write them a thank-you note.

Devotion

What sacrifices have you made for each other? Name the simple sacrifices you could make to express your love.

Habits of the Heart

Even when disagreements are not resolved, some couples never go to sleep unless they say, 'I love you.' Other couples never leave the house without kissing each other good-bye. What habits of the heart could you cultivate to bring you and your partner closer together?

Expressing the Truth

The truth is liberating. If you feel stuck in your relationship, it's often because you are not being entirely honest with yourself and your partner. Whenever you feel at an impasse in your relationship or in your life, ask yourself what the truth is. Begin by saying, 'The truth is _____.' Continue to say, 'The truth is _____.' until you have uncovered the whole truth.

The Devastations of Life

At one time or another, most couples experience the challenges of love and the devastations of life. Through illness, income loss, or problems with children, thoughts of separation or divorce often occur. Express what you would be willing to do to hold the relationship together, for example, counseling, marriage encounter groups, or more time together. List the challenge and the solution.

Becoming Our Best

How does your partner encourage you to grow? Does your partner support you in being your best? Do you support your partner? If not, write about what needs to change.

Dark Night of the Soul

A dark night of the soul is when you temporarily lose faith. Sometimes life gives us more than we think we can bear. Write about a time in your life when you experienced a dark night of the soul. Express your suffering, pain, and sadness.

Favorite Recipes

Write a recipe for something you would like to cook up in your life or for something you are already planning. A sumptuous meal is prepared with the finest ingredients. What ingredients are required to achieve your heart's desire?

Books on Love, Relationships, and Intimacy That Have Inspired Me

Men Are from Mars, Women Are from Venus
by John Gray

Getting the Love You Want
by Harville Hendrix

Keeping the Love You Find
by Harville Hendrix

Books by Barbara De Angelis

A Return to Love
by Marianne Williamson

The Language of Love
by Gary Smalley and John Trent, Ph.D.

The Art and Practice of Loving
by Frank Andrews, Ph.D.

Challenge of the Heart
edited by John Welwood

A Path to Love
by Deepak Chopra

Into the Garden: A Wedding Anthology
(poetry and prose on love and marriage)
edited by Robert Hass and
Stephen Mitchell

How to Forgive When You Don't Know How
by Jaqui Bishop, M.S. and Mary Grunte, R.N.

The Seven Habits of Highly Effective Families
by Steven Covey

Love and Awakening
by John Welwood

To Love and Be Loved
by Sam Keen

The Couple's Comfort Book
by Jennifer Louden

The Conscious Heart
by Gay Hendricks

Living in Love
by Alexandra Stoddard

The Knight in Rusty Armor
by Robert Fisher

The Alchemist
by Paulo Coelho

The Tao of Relationships
by Ray Griggs

Pillow: Exploring the Heart of Eros
by Lily Pond

*The Ten Second Miracle:
Creating Relationship Breakthroughs*
by Gay Hendricks

CELESTIAL ARTS

P.O. Box 7123
Berkeley, CA 94707
e-mail: order@tenspeed.com
website: www.tenspeed.com

Celestial Arts books are distributed in Canada by Ten Speed Canada, in the United Kingdom and Europe by Airlift Books, in New Zealand by Southern Publishers Group, in Australia by Simon & Schuster Australia, in South Africa by Real Books, and in Singapore, Malaysia, Hong Kong and Thailand by Berkeley Books.

Cover design by Shelley Firth
Text design by Greene Design
Cover photograph by Debora Cartwright at The Dark Room in San Carlos
Photographs on pages 40, 41, 54, 55, 76, 77, 98–101 by Debora Cartwright
The photograph on page 94–97 by Cathy Scheer
The sculpture on pages 32–33 by Craig Turner

A HEART & STAR BOOK

Library of Congress Card Catalog Number
98-073592

ISBN 0-89087-972-9

First printing, 1998
Printed in Hong Kong

00 01 02 03 / 6 5 4 3 2 1

For information regarding Rose Offner's books, tapes, lectures, workshops, and consulting arrangements, contact:

FROM THE INSIDE OUT
Rose Offner, c/o Celestial Arts
PO Box 7123,
Berkeley, CA 94707
(510) 538-5074
roseoffner@aol.com
www.roseoffner.com

Other Books by Rose Offner:
Journal to the Soul
Letters to the Soul
Journal to the Soul for Teenagers